MEDIA BIAS

What Is It and Why Does It Matter?

HAL MARCOVITZ

ReferencePoint Press

San Diego, CA

About the Author

Hal Marcovitz graduated from Temple University in Philadelphia with a degree in journalism. He went on to spend thirty years in the print media, working as a newspaper reporter and columnist. He is the author of more than two hundred books for young readers as well as the novels *Painting the White House* and *My Life with Wings*. He makes his home in Chalfont, Pennsylvania.

© 2023 ReferencePoint Press, Inc.
Printed in the United States

For more information, contact:
ReferencePoint Press, Inc.
PO Box 27779
San Diego, CA 92198
www.ReferencePointPress.com

LIBRARY OF CONGRESS CATALOGING-IN-PUBLICATION DATA

Names: Marcovitz, Hal, author.
Title: Media bias : what is it and why does it matter? / by Hal Marcovitz.
Description: San Diego, CA : ReferencePoint Press, Inc., 2023. | Includes
   bibliographical references and index.
Identifiers: LCCN 2022002259 (print) | LCCN 2022002260 (ebook) | ISBN
   9781678203627 (library binding) | ISBN 9781678203634 (ebook)
Subjects: LCSH: Mass media--Objectivity--United States--Juvenile
   literature. | Journalism--Objectivity--United States--Juvenile
   literature.
Classification: LCC P96.O242 U653 2023 (print) | LCC P96.O242 (ebook) |
   DDC 302.230973--dc23/eng/20220316
LC record available at https://lccn.loc.gov/2022002259
LC ebook record available at https://lccn.loc.gov/2022002260

CONTENTS

INTRODUCTION

Media Bias and the Trial of Kyle Rittenhouse

For nearly three weeks in the fall of 2021, the trial of Kyle Rittenhouse dominated the news. A year before, Rittenhouse—then just seventeen years old—was arrested in the homicides of two men and the attempted homicide of a third. The alleged crimes occurred in the summer of 2020 during a chaotic public demonstration in the streets of Kenosha, Wisconsin, against police abuse. The demonstration was prompted when a White Kenosha police officer shot Jacob Blake, a Black man—leaving him paralyzed.

Similar demonstrations had been occurring for months in many American cities as Black citizens and others staged protests against police misconduct. Some of the protests spun out of control. The demonstrations in Kenosha included incidents of vandalism and other violent acts committed by protesters. Watching the chaos unfold was Rittenhouse, a White teenager who lived some 20 miles (32 km) away in Antioch, Illinois. On the night of August 25, Rittenhouse traveled to Kenosha and, armed with an assault rifle, walked into the angry demonstrations unfolding around him. That night Rittenhouse fatally shot two demonstrators and injured a third. All three victims were White. A day later he was arrested and charged with homicide and attempted homicide. If convicted of those charges, the teen faced life in prison.

Rittenhouse testified at his trial. He claimed that he traveled to Kenosha to help protect the homes and businesses of innocent property owners. He also stated that he fired his gun in self-defense—that he feared for his life when he encountered the three individuals whom he shot. After the evidence was presented in the trial, the jury found Rittenhouse not guilty on all charges.

The verdict sparked debate throughout American society. Many people who followed the trial in the news believed Rittenhouse acted as a vigilante, arming himself and taking the law into his own hands. Others believed he had every right under the law to protect himself with deadly force. The issue of race sparked debate as well, as many Black citizens and others suggested that if Rittenhouse had been Black and charged with shooting three White victims, he never would have been acquitted.

Reporters Flock to Kenosha

A lot of that debate was sparked by how the Rittenhouse trial was covered by the news media. Journalists flocked to Kenosha and filled the courtroom. Each day, coverage of the trial was featured in newspapers, radio and TV broadcasts, internet-based news sites, and social media platforms. Along with the news stories reporting the testimony of witnesses, commentators weighed in—giving their opinions on how the case was unfolding. Many of those news reports and commentaries illustrate actual bias or show why people *think* the media is biased.

Shortly after Rittenhouse's arrest and well before the evidence was presented in court, Fox News commentator Laura Ingraham had this to say:

> I don't want to come out and pre-judge the case. I haven't seen all witness interviews . . . [but] I am going to say we can't arrive at a place in our country where law-abiding Americans who are trying to protect themselves and their

property are made into villains. If that's the case, we are going to be in for a really, really long and protracted period of complete chaos and destruction which I don't think the American people want.[1]

Although Ingraham prefaced her remarks by saying the evidence had yet to come out, she still insisted Rittenhouse was innocent.

Others weighed in as well. Following Rittenhouse's arrest—and again, well before the evidence was presented in court—journalist and commentator David A. Love pronounced the young man guilty. He wrote:

Kyle Rittenhouse is a white domestic terrorist who should spend a lifetime in prison. . . . A normal country would react to its own Kyle Rittenhouses with condemnation. But in the land of the free—where a domestic terrorist is a freedom fighter when he fights for white supremacy and a country that continues to oppress and murder Black people—such young thugs are afforded a hero's welcome.[2]

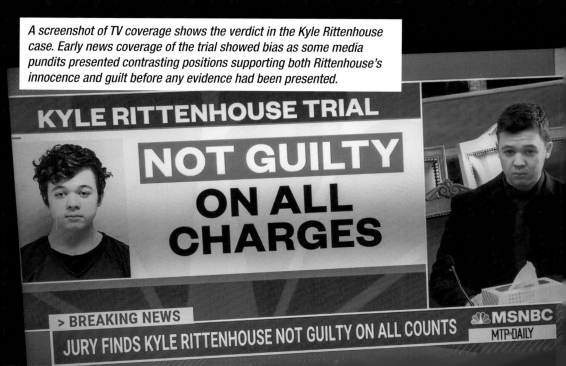

A screenshot of TV coverage shows the verdict in the Kyle Rittenhouse case. Early news coverage of the trial showed bias as some media pundits presented contrasting positions supporting both Rittenhouse's innocence and guilt before any evidence had been presented.

KYLE RITTENHOUSE TRIAL

NOT GUILTY
ON ALL CHARGES

> BREAKING NEWS

JURY FINDS KYLE RITTENHOUSE NOT GUILTY ON ALL COUNTS

MSNBC
MTP-DAILY

Biased Viewpoints Common

The comments by Love and Ingraham illustrate how two members of the media can provide vastly different views of the same event. Henry A. Brechter, editor of AllSides, a media watchdog group, says biased members of the media pounced on the Rittenhouse trial, using it as fodder to push their conceptions of how American culture should be portrayed. Ingraham represented views from the so-called political right—conservative viewpoints in which societal change is generally not welcomed. Love provided views from the political left: liberal (also known as progressive) views insisting that American society is far from inclusive and often favors a privileged class. "The high-profile trial of Kyle Rittenhouse . . . took over the national media this week—and led to clear examples of media bias," wrote Brechter as the trial unfolded. "In general, the left and right are focusing on different aspects of the events in order to underscore their differing narratives about Rittenhouse, and their perspectives of him either as a hero or a criminal."[3]

> "Kyle Rittenhouse is a white domestic terrorist who should spend a lifetime in prison."[2]
>
> —David A. Love, liberal commentator

As the comments by Ingraham and Love illustrate, biased viewpoints have become a routine part of how the media report the news in America. Readers of daily newspapers as well as people who receive their news through radio or TV broadcasts and those who rely on the internet for their news can certainly find straight reporting in those sources. But biased coverage of the news is ever present as well, providing consumers with the challenge of finding truth in the flood of daily news coverage.

CHAPTER ONE

News, Opinion, and Bias: How Do They Differ?

The press has been a part of American culture dating back to colonial days. In 1729 Benjamin Franklin and partner Hugh Meredith purchased the *Pennsylvania Gazette*, a newspaper published in Philadelphia. Under the ownership of Franklin and Meredith, the *Gazette* did more than just report the local news. In the ensuing decades, Franklin and Meredith used the newspaper to advocate for revolution against the British. In 1754 the *Gazette* published a cartoon of a snake chopped into eight slices—each slice representing one of the eight colonies then in existence. The caption for the cartoon said, "Join, or Die." The sketch became a symbol of the campaign to win independence from Great Britain. It took more than two decades, but due in no small part to the advocacy of the *Gazette*, the Declaration of Independence was signed in 1776.

One of the signers was Franklin, who was still serving as publisher of the *Gazette*. In other words, Franklin was hardly the model of a neutral media executive who saw his or her responsibility as providing a fair and unbiased version of the news to readers. Rather, Franklin favored revolution, and he used his newspaper to mold the thinking of his fellow colonists.

Franklin would not be the last member of the American media to offer a biased view of the news to readers. Today media bias is a common element in the information culture. It can be found in the print media—newspapers and magazines—as well as on TV, radio, and internet-based news platforms. While biased media reporting is widespread, there are also many examples of news media making every effort to present fair and accurate reporting. The work of gathering and reporting the news starts with the reporters who are dispatched to cover the news.

Objective Reporting

The backbone of any legitimate news outlet—whether in print, over the radio and TV airwaves, or through an internet portal—is the reporter. It is the responsibility of reporters to gather facts about the stories they plan to write. Typically, they do this by conducting interviews with people involved in the story and, often, by reviewing relevant documents. Once they have gathered the necessary facts and finished with the interviews, they write a straight and unbiased version of the event. For example, a reporter dispatched to the scene of a bank robbery would typically interview witnesses, executives of the bank, and police officers, and then relate the facts of the story to readers, listeners, or viewers. Likewise, a reporter assigned to cover a political campaign would be expected to attend speeches by the candidates, interview potential voters, and talk to independent political analysts such as pollsters in order to craft stories about the campaign.

Essentially, there is no difference between writing stories about bank robberies and political campaigns. The stories are based on the facts gathered by reporters. Those facts are related to readers, listeners, and viewers in a manner that provides useful information as well as makes the story intriguing. A well-told story engages news consumers and makes them want to know more.

Reporters strive to be objective in how they report and write their stories, meaning they must provide all sides of the story. In other words, if a political leader takes a position on an issue, it is the responsibility of the reporter to find a spokesperson with an opposite view—thereby giving both sides to the story.

Reporters are barred from injecting their personal feelings into stories. News stories are generally not written in the narrative technique known as the *first person*, meaning the reporter does not describe events using the pronouns *I* or *me*. In describing the scene of a bank robbery, for example, the reporter would not construct the story by saying, "A witness to the robbery told me. . . . " Every legitimate news organization employs reporters to craft these stories.

Editorials and Columns

Over the years, news outlets have not only offered news stories but also opinions: analyses of the news crafted into viewpoints on how the news affects readers, listeners, and viewers. Some news outlets are dedicated almost entirely to opinion and analysis. The *National Review* is a well-known and highly regarded magazine, published twice a month and read by some seventy-five thousand subscribers. The magazine backs conservative positions on issues ranging from diplomatic relations with other countries to tax issues that affect American citizens. In contrast, the *New Yorker* is a weekly magazine that reaches some 1.2 million readers. The magazine was founded in 1925 to cover the literary, theatrical, and dining culture of the New York City borough of Manhattan, but in modern times it has dived deeply into cultural and political stories and is well known for offering readers progressive interpretations of the stories it covers.

But neither the *New Yorker*, the *National Review*, or similar news outlets can be considered biased in how they present their stories. The writers of the stories provide analyses of the issues based on the facts they glean as they prepare their stories. Spokespersons for all sides of the issues examined in the publications are interviewed. Independent experts are often interviewed. Most impor-

In 1729, Benjamin Franklin purchased the Pennsylvania Gazette, *a newspaper published in Philadelphia. Rather than simply reporting unbiased news, Franklin used the newspaper to advocate for revolution against the British.*

tantly, readers of the *New Yorker* and the *National Review* are well aware of the magazine's reputations and positions on the issues.

When readers pick up their local newspapers or tune to their local radio or TV news broadcasts, it is not unusual for them to find opinions, analyses, and commentaries. For example, in newspapers, readers can find editorials. These are viewpoints expressed by the newspaper's editorial board. Typically, a newspaper's editorial board is composed of senior editors as well as staff members assigned specifically to the editorial page, where their duties include writing editorials and selecting letters to the editor to publish. Usually meeting daily, members of the editorial board may decide to take a position on a public issue, such as a proposed tax increase under consideration by local government leaders. Or the newspaper may endorse a certain candidate for election, encouraging readers to vote for that candidate. The editorials are clearly marked as such and not presented as news. Moreover, the editorial writers base

Going for Shock Value

Some news organizations rely on a form of reporting known as sensationalism to attract readers and viewers and, therefore, earn huge profits for their owners. News organizations that specialize in sensationalism report stories that readers find emotionally shocking. Moreover, though, these news organizations may sensationalize the stories on their own, adding shock value to their reporting. There may be a kernel of truth in the story, but the journalists who cover the stories play up the most shocking aspects of the stories in an effort to touch the emotions of readers.

Shortly after her 2018 marriage to Prince Harry—an heir to the British throne—the actress Meghan Markle often found herself the target of sensationalism. In 2020, for example, many news organizations reported that Markle had once had a love affair with the British actor Simon Rex. The newspapers sold a lot of copies to readers anxious to learn more about Markle's private life—except that soon after the media aired those stories, Rex stepped forward and said they were untrue. Although he and Markle were friends, they were never lovers. Moreover, Rex said, numerous news outlets offered him cash for interviews in which he was told to falsely claim to have had an affair with Markle. Rex said he turned down all the offers, one of which was for $70,000.

their opinions on factual information. In the case of the tax increase, for example, the editorial writers would assess the amount of money the tax is expected to raise and whether that money would be put to good use by the government. If the editorial writers conclude that the tax increase is warranted, they would use the space on the editorial page to advocate for the tax hike.

Newspapers also employ columnists—writers who use space in newspapers to provide their opinions on the news. Many of these columns can be found on the so-called op-ed pages— literally, the pages opposite the editorial pages. But columnists can be found elsewhere as well—on the local news page, giving opinions on events that impact local communities. Or on the sports page, providing commentary on how well the local teams may be competing. Or even on the entertainment page, urging readers to see certain movies—or to save their money and not spend it on movies the entertainment critics do not deem worthy of the price of admission. Today most newspapers have internet platforms, and columnists can be found there as well. Internet-based news outlets that do not feature print versions also employ columnists. On radio and TV, commentators fill those roles, speaking their minds about current issues, assessing the performances of local teams, and providing reviews of newly released films.

"A reporter—which I was for most of my career—gathers information from a variety of sources and presents it in as balanced and unbiased a manner as possible."[4]

—Carrie Seidman, columnist for the *Daytona Beach News-Journal*

Columnists and on-air commentators are expected to base their opinions on facts. They are expected to do the work of reporters—interviewing participants, examining documents, and tapping other sources. They are expected to construct their analyses and opinions based on factual and trustworthy information. In fact, most columnists spend at least a few years as reporters—proving their mettle as news gatherers—before they are given opportunities by their editors to write columns. Says Carrie Seidman, a columnist for the *Daytona Beach News-Journal* in Florida:

A reporter—which I was for most of my career—gathers information from a variety of sources and presents it in as balanced and unbiased a manner as possible, the goal being for the reader to end up with no idea of where that reporter's own feelings may lie.

A columnist abides by the same information gathering rules, but is not only free to express personal opinion, but encouraged and given great latitude to do so. . . .

Columns are, by nature, one-sided. Columnists are not required to be dispassionate, or even balanced. They are also given more leeway stylistically, by, for example, being allowed to use "I," forgo formal titles and take whatever tone exemplifies their personality, be it sarcastic, humorous snarky, or outraged.[4]

Many Forms of Bias

Still, despite the best efforts of many news outlets to ensure that stories, editorials, columns, and on-air commentaries are based on indisputable facts, bias does manage to find its way into news coverage. Bias in the media can be found in many forms. Members of the media pushing biased viewpoints are not likely to base their reporting on hard facts. Rather, their reporting is based mostly on their own interpretations of events—twisting the truth to fit their worldviews. Some members of the media push narratives that fall into the category of "fake news"—events that are completely fabricated yet represented by biased journalists as bona fide stories. Typically, fake news stories are presented with the intention of belittling viewpoints that oppose those of the journalist or media outlet pushing the fake story.

Biased reporting does not strive for objectivity. Biased journalists are not likely to seek the other side of a story. Instead, they base their reporting solely on the comments made by the newsmakers

Biased journalists are not likely to seek the other side of a story. Instead, they base their reporting solely on the comments made by the newsmakers they choose to interview.

they choose to interview. Or, if they do seek out opposing viewpoints, it is likely the spokespersons they select for the interviews will be subjected to relentless badgering designed to ridicule their positions. This type of harsh interview technique is a common tactic employed by biased cable TV news journalists. One of the most noted examples of this technique occurred in 2013 when conservative Fox News host Sean Hannity berated Keith Ellison, a liberal member of the US House of Representatives from Minnesota, about the failure of Congress to agree on cuts in the federal budget. Flustered by Ellison's refusal to place the blame for the budget impasse on then-president Barack Obama, Hannity told Ellison, "Congressman, you are a total waste of time."[5]

Bias on the Right

Biased reporting can also be driven by the pursuit of a healthy profit margin. Indeed, University of Tampa economics professor Cagdas Agirdas, who has studied the roots of media bias, has found that bias is invariably driven by a desire by media owners to earn healthy profits. In other words, media outlets are willing to provide news consumers with slanted reporting knowing that these biased stories will appeal to the worldviews of those consumers. "I frequently hear people complain about how biased the media is, and I have always wondered why the news outlets that are perceived to be the most biased also enjoy the largest viewership [and] readership,"[6] says Agirdas.

A 2018 study by the Florida-based Knight Foundation—which studies media-related issues in American society—found that the news outlet most Americans consider to be biased is Fox News, the cable TV network established by billionaire Rupert Murdoch. Fox News features numerous commentators who espouse conservative viewpoints largely in line with the politics of the Republican Party. The Knight Foundation study, which was performed with the assistance of the polling firm Gallup, found that 90 percent of the people it polled believe that Fox News is biased.

It is easy to see why Fox News espouses a predominantly conservative slant to the news: it is seeking viewers who regard themselves as politically conservative. Therefore, the more viewers who tune in to Fox News—to hear news related to them the way they want to hear it—the more the network can charge the companies that advertise on Fox News. Traditionally, in TV as well as in other media, advertising rates are based on the number of viewers or readers reached by those outlets.

It is a business plan that, at least for Fox News, has been highly successful. In 2021 the news show *Tucker Carlson Tonight*, hosted by conservative commentator Tucker Carlson, was reported to have reached 2.9 million viewers a night—the largest audience for any cable TV news and commentary show. Given some of Carlson's characterizations of major issues and events, his viewpoints could be considered biased. For example, on a telecast aired in September 2021, Carlson suggested (without evidence) that the administration of President Joe Biden planned to permit hundreds of thousands of immigrants to cross the border into America. The goal of this plan, Carlson stated, was to grant them citizenship and voting rights so that they would elect Democrats and cast Republicans out of office. "Once they get here the Biden administration plans to give them voting rights," Carlson told his viewers. As images of people seeking entry at the US-Mexico border flashed on-screen, Carlson continued, "That's in the works right now. So, the people you just saw on your screen could very well be choosing your president at some point down the road. . . . This is an attempt to change the demographics of the United States in order to give permanent power to the Democratic Party."[7]

In fact, the Biden administration has no plans to permit immigrants to freely enter the country. To gain permission to enter the United States, immigrants must undergo a review process by fed-

Each day, millions of Americans turn to online news sites and social media feeds for updates on unfolding current events. What they see, hear, or read can vary immensely, depending on the source.

eral officials and obtain the necessary documents proving they have followed legal channels when they arrive on American soil. Still, Carlson's biased viewpoint of the issue of immigration found traction among the typical Fox News viewer, whose dedication to the network is important to maintaining advertising revenue.

Independent fact-checkers have routinely found Carlson's assertions to be based on false premises—in other words, fake news. For example, following the January 6, 2021, insurrection at the US Capitol, when supporters of President Donald Trump stormed into the Capitol in an effort to overturn the results of the 2020 presidential election, Carlson made a bizarre suggestion on his show. He said that the nation's chief law enforcement agency, the Federal Bureau of Investigation, organized and engineered the insurrection. Carlson's provocative statements often veer so far beyond what is considered unbiased reporting that they actually become news—prompting other news outlets to look into his accusations. For instance, after Carlson's reporting on the origins of the Capitol attack, the cable news network CNN reported,

"The underlying [report] was nothing more than a conspiratorial web of unproven claims, half-truths and inaccurate drivel about perceived bombshells."[8]

Bias on the Left

Bias (stemming from a desire to attract viewers and thus profits) can also be found in news coverage by left-leaning news media. Trailing just behind *Tucker Carlson Tonight* in the ratings war is *The Rachel Maddow Show*, a political commentary program featured nightly on the MSNBC cable TV network. The show is hosted by liberal firebrand Rachel Maddow, whose views often mirror those of the most liberal wing of the Democratic Party. In 2021 Maddow's show reported 2.5 million nightly viewers. The 2018 Knight Foundation study found that viewers regarded MSNBC as almost as biased as Fox News, with 86 percent of people it polled believing the network's telecasts are biased.

> "The underlying [report] was nothing more than a conspiratorial web of unproven claims, half-truths and inaccurate drivel about perceived bombshells."[8]
>
> —CNN

Like Carlson, Maddow has been criticized for biased reporting. In 2017, for example, she enthusiastically hyped what she claimed to be a major scoop: she had unearthed Trump's tax records. Presidents have traditionally released their tax records for public scrutiny, but Trump, a billionaire real estate developer who was elected in 2016, steadfastly refused to do so. His refusal to release his tax records fueled speculation among his political opponents that he was hiding facts about his personal income that might reveal illegal activity.

As the show opened that evening, Maddow told her viewers, "It's been a little bit of a hullabaloo around here this evening, I apologize for being flustered. In just a second we're going to show you exactly what it is we've got."[9] Maddow kept her viewers dangling for several minutes into the evening's broadcast until she finally got

Bias at the Supermarket

So-called supermarket tabloids have been a part of American culture for decades. Typically, they can be found in the checkout aisles of supermarkets, luring shoppers with bizarre headlines accusing movie stars and other celebrities of various indiscretions. Largely published for entertainment value, few readers would admit to taking the news in supermarket tabloids like the *National Enquirer* seriously.

In 2016, though, the *Enquirer* turned decidedly political in its news coverage, targeting Democratic presidential candidate Hillary Clinton. For example, during the campaign one *Enquirer* headline announced that Clinton had just six months to live. There was no truth to the story. Nevertheless, the headline on page 1 of the *Enquirer* reporting Clinton's supposed health problems read, "Hillary Clinton: White House Dream Is Over!" Eventually, the facts behind the *Enquirer*'s campaign were revealed: David Pecker, the chief executive officer of the company that owns the *Enquirer*, was a close personal friend of Donald Trump, Clinton's opponent in the 2016 election, and Pecker was using the *Enquirer* to advance Trump's candidacy.

Quoted in Media Bias/Fact Check, "*National Enquirer*," September 16, 2021. https://mediabiasfact check.com.

to the big reveal, which was not much of anything. Maddow produced two pages from the president's 2005 tax records—which ultimately revealed very little about Trump's personal financial history. Said media critic Willa Paskin:

> The longer Maddow went on, ever deeper into a conspiratorial thicket, the clearer it became that whatever tax returns Maddow had, they weren't as juicy as the ones she was talking about. If she had anything that damning, she would have shared them from the start. TV is a ratings game, but an entire episode about highly damaging tax returns is just as likely to get you great ratings as milking the possibility that you have highly damaging tax returns. . . . Maddow even went so far as to hold the tax returns back until after the first commercial break, as if

we were watching an episode of *The Bachelor* and not a matter of national importance—because we weren't, in fact, watching a matter of national importance, just a cable news show trying to set a ratings record.[10]

The Hallmarks of Fair and Unbiased Reporting

Each day, millions of Americans turn to TV, radio, online news sites, and social media feeds for updates on unfolding current events. What they see or hear or read can vary immensely, depending on the source. Fair and unbiased reporting depends on facts—not rumors or conjecture. It does not base stories on a single source. It strives for objectivity. It seeks comment from a variety of sources, including those with differing views. It clearly labels news as news and opinion as opinion. It does not mix the two. These are some of the hallmarks of fair and unbiased news reporting—and they are worth remembering.

CHAPTER TWO

How Does Bias Affect News Consumers?

After nearly a year of living under the threat of the deadly COVID-19 pandemic, Americans and citizens of other countries finally found relief in the spring of 2021 when vaccines to prevent the illness became widely available. By then the COVID-19 death toll in America stood at more than five hundred thousand victims.

The vaccines were produced by three pharmaceutical companies and eventually offered free to all Americans over age five. Millions of Americans lined up for the shots. Millions more did not. In fact, in March 2022 the Centers for Disease Control and Prevention (CDC) reported that about 19 percent of eligible Americans—some 35 million people— had not been vaccinated.

A December 2021 poll conducted by the US Census Bureau found that most people who have refused to get the vaccinations simply do not believe the shots are necessary. CDC officials have consistently stated that vaccines are the best way to avoid serious illness and death from the COVID-19 virus. This has not changed the minds of those who have chosen not to get vaccinated.

Influencing Vaccination Decisions

Many of these individuals have likely seen or heard stories in the media questioning or denying the accuracy and authenticity of scientific studies confirming the safety and effectiveness of the vaccines. They have probably also heard or read that the vaccination program is a government-sponsored plot to deny Americans the right to make their own decisions about their health care. Said Brian Kilmeade, cohost of the popular Fox News morning show *Fox & Friends*:

> They're going to knock on your door, they're going to demand that you take it, and they're going to give you a third shot. It's unbelievable how offensive [the Biden] administration is getting with a pandemic that is clearly on the run. We're doing better than any other country. Almost 60–70 percent of this country has taken two shots, and yet this administration is panicking and infiltrating our lives.[11]

Kilmeade did not present any facts to back up his assertions. He did not seek comment from anyone in the Biden administration. In fact, there has been no door-knocking campaign conducted by the federal government to force Americans to get vaccinated or boosted. And despite Kilmeade's assertion that the United States is doing a better job than other countries in vaccinating its citizens, the facts suggest otherwise. According to the United Kingdom–based Global Change Data Lab's Our World in Data project, the vaccination rate in the United States is just fifteenth best in the world. And by March 2022 the United States had experienced nearly 1 million COVID-related deaths—more than any other nation on earth.

Biased reporting and commentary about vaccines (and about the virus in general) may have cost thousands of lives. By early 2022—nearly a year after the vaccines became

> "We're doing better than any other country. . . . And yet this administration is panicking and infiltrating our lives."[11]
>
> —Brian Kilmeade, *Fox & Friends* cohost

People who resist COVID vaccinations were likely influenced by media reports questioning their safety and effectiveness.

widely available—another three hundred thousand people had died after being infected with the COVID-19 virus. And, according to the CDC, the vast majority of the fatalities were among people who had not been vaccinated.

Derailing a Presidential Candidate

Biased reporting, especially when it is based on fabricated information, can impact life in other ways as well. The 1970s provide a case in point. For many years one of the most influential newspapers in the country was the *Manchester Union Leader* in New Hampshire. Every four years New Hampshire is the site of the first presidential primary, meaning candidates for president flock to the state for several weeks prior to the primary and vie for attention in the local media. For decades, the *Union Leader* was owned by William Loeb, whose conservative positions were reflected in the news pages of the newspaper. Loeb was not above using the *Union Leader* to derail the candidacies of presidential contenders he opposed.

Media Bias and Black Protests

A 2020 study on how the media covers protests by Black activists found that journalists tend to build their stories by interviewing officials of law enforcement and other governmental leaders more so than by seeking interviews with protesters. The study, by Indiana University journalism professor Danielle Kilgo, looked at more than seven hundred news stories written about Black protests and found that only 8 percent could be regarded as fairly balanced. In 30 percent of the stories, journalists featured interviews with officials of law enforcement and government only; in 23 percent of the stories, their reports included interviews with protesters only. Moreover, the study found that in 39 percent of the stories, neither side was interviewed.

Kilgo says a reason for the bias may be found in the tight deadlines imposed on reporters to produce their stories. Given so little time, she says, it is often easier for reporters to pick up their phone and get official statements from city or police officials than it is for them to traipse into city neighborhoods in search of protest leaders. "On tight deadlines, reporters may default to official sources for statements and data," she says. "This gives authorities more control of narrative framing. This practice especially becomes an issue for movements like Black Lives Matter that are countering the claims of police and other officials."

Danielle Kilgo, "Riot or Resistance? The Way the Media Frames the Unrest in Minneapolis Will Shape the Public's View of Protest," NiemanLab, May 30, 2020. www.niemanlab.org.

Most famously, in 1972 the *Union Leader* published what was later found to be a phony letter, purportedly written by an acquaintance of Senator Edmund Muskie. According to the letter, the senator from Maine was reported to have belittled Americans of French Canadian descent—a large population of whom resided in New Hampshire. At the time, Muskie was a candidate for the Democratic nomination for president. Shortly after the letter was published, Muskie publicly—and tearfully—denounced the *Union Leader* for printing lies. The letter, although false, had inflicted serious injury to his campaign, and the widespread news coverage that followed essentially killed his candidacy.

How Bias Seeps into Editorial Decisions

How to cover newsworthy events such as crimes, major fires, and environmental threats is likely the subject of conversation in nearly every newsroom in the country. Conversations of this nature occur every day between reporters and editors or producers. When a news event occurs, the editors at a news organization make decisions on the importance of the event, which will determine how it will be covered and ultimately featured in that day's package of news. For example, a traffic accident on a major highway may prompt a local TV station to dispatch a camera crew to film a few seconds of footage for that evening's newscast, but a major fire in the city may prompt the station to dispatch numerous camera crews and reporters to film emergency responders fighting the fire and interview witnesses at the scene. The decisions made by editors and producers on how the stories are covered are largely based on their experiences as journalists in gauging the importance of the stories to news consumers.

But not all stories are as clear-cut as highway traffic accidents or major fires. News value, or the perceived importance of a given story, can be misjudged by reporters and editors or producers who fall victim to their own personal biases. This bias is not necessarily intentional or malicious. Journalists, like other individuals, view events through the lens of their own experiences. And sometimes they miss a story of real significance to people and communities because they have no personal context for understanding its importance. This too is a form of media bias.

A prime example of this occurred in 2013 when officials in Flint, Michigan, decided to use the Flint River as a water supply. For decades, Flint had been buying water from the nearby city of Detroit, but municipal officials sought a cheaper source of water. They planned to build a new pipeline from Lake Huron; in the meantime, they elected to draw water from the river that flowed through their city. A number of environmental studies had questioned the decision to draw water from the Flint River, finding that the river was highly polluted. Flint city officials insisted there was nothing wrong with the water. In 2014 the changeover to the Flint River was made—piping the highly corrosive water through aging pipes into the households of the city's largely Black and low-income population.

Flint residents protested the change, and these protests were well covered in the local media. But city officials found it easy to ignore the local editorials, columnists, and commentators who called attention to the environmental hazards. As for the national media—the network TV newscasts, cable TV news crews, and influential big-city newspapers in New York City and Washington, DC—the Flint story was largely ignored.

Within three years a dozen citizens of Flint had died and nearly one hundred more were sickened—their illnesses attributed to lead and other toxic substances leaching from the aging pipes into their drinking water. In 2017 five Flint officials were criminally charged in the deaths. By 2022 another four government officials

In 2013, officials of Flint, Michigan decided to use the Flint River (pictured) as a water source for city residents. Residents protested the decision citing pollution studies of the river, but national media largely ignored the controversy.

had been charged in the case; all had yet to come to trial. As for the residents of the city, they were told to stop drinking water out of the taps in their homes and to drink bottled water only.

National Media Ignores Crisis in Flint

Many critics believe that if the national media had been drawn to the Flint story at the outset, the city officials might have acted differently. Says Margaret Sullivan, an editor at the *New York Times*:

> Imagine if the *Times* really had taken on the Flint outrage with energy and persistence. . . . With its powerful pulpit and reach, the *Times* could have held public officials accountable and prevented human suffering. That's what journalistic watchdogs are supposed to do. . . . If the *Times* had kept the pressure on the Flint story, the resulting journalism . . . would have made a real difference to the people of Flint, who were in serious need of a powerful ally.[12]

One reason the story was ignored by national media organizations could be attributed to bias. It was not a bias based on a desire to push a liberal or conservative political agenda. Rather, this type of bias was harbored in the minds of editors and producers who did not have any real connection to or interest in Michigan's economically depressed, mostly Black neighborhoods or their residents. Editors and producers in the national media failed to realize the dangers faced by the residents of Flint, who were being forced to drink polluted water.

Media critics have cited the lack of diversity in news organizations as contributing to biased thinking when it comes to determining news value. Indeed, according to a study by the

> "With its powerful pulpit and reach, the *Times* could have held public officials accountable and prevented human suffering."[12]
>
> —Margaret Sullivan, *New York Times* editor

Bias While Covering the Home Team

Sportswriters assigned to cover their hometown teams often find themselves in difficult predicaments. Assigned to report on how well those teams compete, they nevertheless know that many of their readers are rooting for the home teams. And while many sportswriters are willing to criticize the players and coaches when those teams do poorly, the sportswriters do know their readers and listeners want to see good news about those teams.

A University of Michigan study found that sportswriters often fall into bias while reporting about their home teams. The study reported the results of a 2003 National Hockey League game in which the Detroit Red Wings defeated the Colorado Avalanche. The study pointed out that the headline in a *Denver Post* story reported, "Injury Begins Avs' Tumble," suggesting the loss was due to injuries sustained by Avalanche players. Meanwhile, the headline in the *Detroit Free Press* reported, "Wings Are Too Much for Avalanche," suggesting that the Red Wings simply outplayed the Avalanche. Wrote college journalism professors Scott Reinardy and Wayne Wanta, "The division between being a supporter of a team and an unbiased reporter is sometimes so narrow that you can hear a sportswriter quietly—or not so quietly—cheer between paragraphs while writing a story."

Scott Reinardy and Wayne Wanta, *The Essentials of Sports Reporting and Writing*. New York: Routledge, 2015, p. 222.

American Society of News Editors, in 2016—at the height of the crisis in Flint—just 17 percent of the employees of American newsrooms were Black, Latino, or Asian. The study suggested that the vast majority of editors, producers, and other influential members of news staffs failed to understand the gravity of the crisis on the low-income and minority population of Flint. In a report about the Flint water crisis news coverage, the media watchdog group Shorenstein Center on Media, Politics and Public Policy at Harvard University noted:

> Newspapers and networks missed the many months of people showing up at city hall and meetings to complain about the water and the rashes and illnesses. . . . In a city

57 percent African-American, 37 percent white, and 40 percent poor, the media missed a story of citizen action that cut across racial and class lines to complain about, and campaign against, the use of Flint River water.[13]

Alex Jones and Infowars

News media bias has real-world effects. This can be seen in media coverage of the Flint water crisis. Bias can be seen most clearly in some internet-based news platforms whose owners have no credentials that would qualify them as legitimate journalists. Many of these news sites are clearly biased, basing their news coverage, analyses, and opinions on information that is either completely false or at least colored to provide false conclusions by readers.

Perhaps no news website fits that mold more than Infowars, owned by ultra-conservative radio talk show host Alex Jones. For example, a recent story featured on Infowars included reports on a secret plot within the US government to trigger a civil war in America. Another story claimed that President Joe Biden, who turned seventy-nine in 2021, is suffering from dementia—a disease that robs elderly victims of their memories, making it difficult for them to perform normal, everyday functions. In fact, Biden is not suffering from dementia, nor is there any secret plot being planned within the depths of the federal government to trigger a civil war. Says the New York City–based national civil rights group Anti-Defamation League:

> Alex Jones is a right-wing American radio host and prolific anti-government conspiracy theorist. Jones rose from public-access television obscurity to national prominence by promoting paranoid allegations against the US government and an alleged shadowy, power-hungry New World Order. . . . Based in Austin, Texas, Jones boasts

a national audience, thanks to his radio show, which is broadcast on 100 stations nationwide, and his [website] Infowars . . . where his many specious claims are presented, in multimedia format, as "news."[14]

Despite the denunciations by the Anti-Defamation League and similar groups, Jones has found an audience that is anxious to engage with his biased views of the news. According to the San Francisco, California–based internet analytics firm Quantcast, the Infowars website attracts more than 3.3 million visitors each month. Many of them have been steered to the website by Tucker Carlson, who insists that Jones's stories are more factually accurate than stories reported by other well-known news organizations. "Jones is often mocked for his flamboyance but the truth is he has been a far better guide to reality in recent years,"[15] Carlson told the nearly 3 million viewers who tuned in to his Fox News show in December 2021.

One of Jones's followers was twenty-eight-year-old Edgar M. Welch of Salisbury, North Carolina. In 2016 Jones published a bizarre story on his website alleging that a popular pizza restaurant in Washington, DC, was in fact the headquarters of a child prostitute trafficking ring headed by leaders of the federal government. The Pizzagate story, as it came to be known, was a complete fabrication. And yet, believing every word of Jones's reporting, Welch traveled to Washington, convinced he was on a mission to save the victims of the prostitution ring. "I can't let you grow up in a world that's so corrupt by evil without at least standing up for you and for other children just like you,"[16] Welch told his two young daughters shortly before leaving for Washington. Armed with a military-style rifle, Welch entered

> "[Alex] Jones rose from public-access television obscurity to national prominence by promoting paranoid allegations against the US government and an alleged shadowy, power-hungry New World Order."[14]
>
> —Anti-Defamation League

News website Infowars is owned by ultra-conservative radio talk show host Alex Jones (shown with bullhorn). The site has a clear bias and often bases its articles and opinions on false or misleading information.

the restaurant and opened fire. Luckily, no one was struck by his shots. As for Welch, he was arrested and ultimately served three years in prison.

Impacting People's Lives

Bias in the media often has a direct impact on people's lives. It can lead to dangerous behavior, as when Welch opened fire in a restaurant to stop a nonexistent child prostitution ring or when rioters stormed the Capitol in response to repeated false claims—by politicians and some members of the news media—of election fraud. Or, as happened in Flint, media bias resulted in scant national coverage of an unfolding health crisis—a crisis that might have been addressed sooner if influential media had paid closer attention. Biased reporting can also lead people not to act in their own best interests. Many of those who rejected COVID-19 vaccination because of biased news reports may have paid for this inaction with their lives.

CHAPTER THREE

Bias in the New Media

During the first two decades of the twenty-first century, as more and more readers turned away from print media, many of them found their news on the internet. In addition to websites created by print publications such as the *New York Times* and *Washington Post*, as well as well-regarded internet-only news sites such as Slate and Vox, other news outlets emerged on the web. Unlike Slate and Vox, though, these sites were established by people with no background in journalism.

Many of these individuals were bloggers, purporting to report the news but doing virtually none of the work involved in actually gathering the news. For the most part, bloggers do not attend press conferences, call sources, pore through documents, or do any of the actual chores ordinarily required to build their stories. Rather, they typically post their own versions of stories they read elsewhere—coloring their reports with their own ideas, analyses, and of course, biases.

Podcasts have also become a popular online vehicle for news and commentary. Many legitimate news organizations—among them National Public Radio, NBC News, and the *New York Times*—feature their content in the form of podcasts. But some podcasts have emerged as another platform for biased reporting.

Podcasts and blogs are part of a new direction in the provision of news known as the new media: News that is available through internet access only. And while there are legitimate online-only news platforms, the internet offers easy access to anyone wishing to provide their own version of the news. Indeed, for the price of a website that typically costs no more than a few hundred dollars a year, anybody can provide whatever content he or she desires. This applies to retailers offering to sell goods, athletic leagues announcing their schedules, and local governments advising motorists which roads are closed due to repairs. It also includes bloggers who use their sites to report news stories to reflect their personal agendas—whatever those agendas might be.

Biased Bloggers

One popular blogger is Wayne Dupree. According to the biography on his blog, Dupree graduated from high school in Baltimore, Maryland, in 1986 and soon enlisted in the US Air Force. Following his discharge from the service, Dupree worked as a website designer. In 2013 Dupree started writing his blog. The biography does not cite any formal training in journalism or the techniques of professional news gathering. In addition to posting his own blog entries, Dupree uses his website to post stories written by other contributors.

The website features deeply conservative views of the news, frequently targeting Democratic Party leaders such as President Joe Biden. For example, in March 2022 Biden spoke at a reception in the White House marking Equal Pay Day—a public awareness event that calls attention to the inequities in salaries for women and men. Historically speaking, men have often earned higher wages for the same jobs held by women. During the event, Biden committed a verbal gaffe. He pointed out that Vice President Kamala Harris could not attend the event because her spouse, Doug Emhoff, had contracted COVID-19. "There's been a little change in arrangement of who is on the stage because of the first lady's husband contracting COVID,"[17] Biden said. In fact, Harris is not the First Lady—a title reserved for the spouse of the president.

One of Dupree's writers, Sophie O'Hara, jumped on what was obviously a misstatement by the president. In her blog post on Dupree's website, she declared that Biden suffers from dementia. "The entire moment was awkward, and of course, the crowd has to laugh, what else are they supposed to do?" O'Hara wrote. "It's uncomfortable watching a man with dementia struggle on the world's stage."[18]

In composing her blog post, O'Hara did not interview participants who attended the Equal Pay Day event to report on their reactions to the president's gaffe. Nor did she consult with the White House physician to determine whether the president suffers from dementia—a mental illness that often afflicts the elderly, causing a loss of memory. In truth, Biden, who was seventy-nine at the time of the event, does not suffer from dementia. Certainly, though, by calling attention to the president's innocent gaffe and declaring that it is clear he suffers from dementia, Dupree's writer was providing a biased account of the event marking Equal Pay Day.

The internet offers easy access to anyone wishing to provide their own version of the news. For no more than a few hundred dollars a year, podcasters or bloggers can launch platforms and provide whatever content they wish.

Comparing Trump to Hitler and Mussolini

The internet features biased liberal bloggers as well. For example, in the liberal blog known as Xplicit News, blogger Glen Reaux has compared former president Donald Trump to Adolf Hitler and Benito Mussolini. Their actions led to World War II and the deaths of more 70 million civilians and members of the military among the dozens of countries that were drawn into the war. Reaux writes:

> Trump-ism, the sociopolitical phenomenon that is poisoning the very core of our political system is not a recent phenomenon. Germany and Italy suffered from the same disease in the thirties which led to the rise of Benito Mussolini, [Adolf] Hitler, and the Nazi Party. These so-called charismatic leaders including Trump share many of the same personality traits; acting impulsively, avoiding conformity to social norms and expectations, regularly engaging in lies and deception, disregard for safety, irresponsible behavior, a lack of remorse, irritability, and aggressiveness.[19]

Trump's policies and positions as president—ranging from his desire to build a wall along the US-Mexico border to deter illegal immigration to his refusal to denounce White nationalists who advocated violence against others—sparked anger across the liberal community. But in 2020 Trump was defeated for reelection and left office—albeit grudgingly—while making the baseless charge that his political enemies conspired to steal the election from him. And while his rhetoric is regarded as prompting the January 6, 2021, riot at the US Capitol by thousands of his supporters, the riot was eventually put down and the

"Trump-ism, the sociopolitical phenomenon that is poisoning the very core of our political system is not a recent phenomenon. Germany and Italy suffered from the same disease in the thirties which led to the rise of Benito Mussolini, [Adolf] Hitler, and the Nazi Party."[19]

—Glen Reaux, blogger

Why Do People Believe Biased News Reporting?

Dan Bongino's Facebook page counts more than 4.8 million followers. Bongino also produces a popular podcast. Though his Facebook page does not mention any journalism background, Bongino regularly reports on political events. In early 2022, for instance, he posted a portion of his podcast on his Facebook page in which he alleged that Joe Biden's son, Hunter Biden, has accepted bribes from a Chinese entrepreneur. The story offers no facts or evidence to support this claim. Nor does it seek comment from the individuals said to be involved.

Studies into why people are drawn to biased commentaries such as this have concluded that people seek out news on the internet—and particularly on social media—in which the reporting supports their worldviews. But also, according to Massachusetts Institute of Technology psychologist David Rand, people who readily accept what they read on social media are either too busy or too lazy to properly assess what they are reading. If they took the time to consider whether the facts support the accusations they read, Rand says, they might truly see bias. "Our findings suggest that getting people to reason more is a good thing," he says. "When you're on social media, stop and think."

Quoted in Kirsten Weir, "Why We Fall for Fake News: Hijacked Thinking or 'Laziness'?," American Psychological Association, February 11, 2020. www.apa.org.

perpetrators arrested. In contrast, Hitler and Mussolini served as dictators, ordering the murders of their political enemies, incarcerating millions of their countries' citizens in concentration camps, and ultimately sparking a global conflict that cost tens of millions of lives. As much loathing as Reaux and other liberals may harbor toward Trump, Reaux's comparison of a democratically elected American president to two of history's most vicious dictators could be regarded as a biased viewpoint. Says Paul Thornton, a columnist for the *Los Angeles Times*, "We know that Trump is no Hitler or Mussolini because we can look back at the full arc of those dictatorships and see the destruction and mass murder that resulted."[20]

According to his biography on the Xplicit News website, Reaux is a retired insurance company executive. If he received any training in legitimate journalism, he did not include it on the biography he posted on his website. His comments comparing Trump to two of history's most evil dictators would suggest he does lack a background in the techniques of responsible journalism.

Bloggers like Reaux and Dupree provide biased analyses of the news because they want people to read their blogs. In other words, Reaux, Dupree, and other biased bloggers provide slanted versions of the news for the same reason that Rachel Maddow and Tucker Carlson provide biased interpretations of the news on their cable TV shows—to attract followers.

According to Aaron Wall, an expert in search engine optimization—techniques that websites employ to draw viewers—bias is a key method of drawing in visitors on the internet. He says, "Bias is talked about as though it is a bad thing, but many of the most popular media outlets, websites, and social networks are popular precisely because they are biased. People are more inclined to believe, pay attention to, and syndicate things that

Trump was defeated by Joe Biden for reelection in 2020, but continuously made the baseless charge that his political enemies conspired to steal the election from him. His rhetoric is regarded as prompting the January 6, 2021, riot at the US Capitol (pictured).

reinforce their current worldview. And people are more likely to respond to things they sharply disagree with."[21]

Monetizing Bias

Spreading their worldviews may be a major motivation for bloggers, but many bloggers also hope to monetize their blogs. In other words, they hope to earn income from their internet commentaries. Some bloggers establish paywalls—charging fees that must be paid by readers in order to access their blogs. Popular blogs that draw thousands of views a day often attract advertisers who pay for the privilege of selling products to the blogger's fans. Or bloggers offer their own products for sale—such as e-books and print books they have self-published. Bloggers who emerge as true superstars in the blogosphere might even receive offers to do on-air commentaries for cable TV networks. Dupree, for example, appears regularly as a commentator on Fox News. (Dupree's website also offers an online store, where fans can buy T-shirts, baseball caps, coffee mugs, and other items proclaiming their support for Dupree.)

Podcasters have a different and more direct route toward monetizing their commentators. Anybody can post a podcast on a website, but to earn substantial income from the podcast, the commentary must be carried by a popular podcast platform such as Apple Podcasts, Spotify, Google Podcasts, and Stitcher. Once the podcaster builds a substantial audience, he or she can offer it to these platforms. If it is picked up, the podcaster can earn a portion of the subscription price listeners pay for access to the platforms.

One of the most popular politically oriented podcasts is Chapo Trap House. Its hosts provide decidedly bi-

> "Bias is talked about as though it is a bad thing, but many of the most popular media outlets, websites, and social networks are popular precisely because they are biased."[21]
>
> —Aaron Wall, search engine optimization expert

The Future of Blogging

In the future, it may become more difficult for many bloggers to spread their messages. The reason is that Google—by far the most-used search engine—is toughening its standards on what can be regarded as legitimate sources of news. For years, anybody with the wherewithal to purchase a web domain could immediately begin to blog, and that blog would show up in Google's search engine listings. In other words, if a reader entered the term "liberal commentary" in the Google search engine, numerous blogs written by liberal authors would surface in the results.

But that standard is changing. Google is known to be applying a standard it calls E-A-T to its search engine. The abbreviation stands for "expertise, authoritativeness, and trustworthiness." Google has developed software that will assess whether the bloggers' credentials qualify them to comment on their chosen topics. It means that a blogger with no background in journalism or political discourse who writes about political topics would likely not show up very high in Google's search engine results. Says Nichehelper, an advisory service for website owners, "To do well with the E-A-T part of Google's [software], you need to show to Google that you are an authority on the subject you are blogging about."

Nichehelper, "The Future of Blogging After 2021—Raising the Stakes," 2021. https://nichehelper.com.

ased commentaries aimed at Republican political leaders as well as Democratic leaders whom they perceive as falling short of true progressive ideals. And while the podcast certainly dives deeply into political topics, its hosts do not interview political leaders to gain insight into their actions. Moreover, the Chapo Trap House hosts do not attend press conferences, nor do they study reports issued by governmental agencies or independent scholars that would help shed light on politically divisive issues—all activities that objective reporters or legitimate columnists or commentators would pursue.

The podcast first gained popularity during 2016 when the hosts backed the candidacy of Senator Bernie Sanders of Vermont. Sanders was seeking the Democratic nomination for president. Among Sanders's positions were free college tuition, free medical care for all citizens, and heavy taxes imposed on the wealthy. Sanders went on to lose the nomination to Hillary Clinton, who ultimately lost the general election to Trump.

In the years following the 2016 election, Chapo Trap House has remained extremely popular with progressives. According to the website Graphtreon, which tracks revenue produced by podcasts, each Chapo Trap House podcast draws some thirty-seven thousand listeners, earning its hosts nearly $2 million a year. Meanwhile, the Chapo Trap House hosts also perform live shows—essentially, in-person versions of their podcasts—and have published books as well. One of the podcast's former hosts, Virgil Texas, says the podcast is popular specifically because of its bias. He says, "It's a common experience to be someone with a crappy job who does not have an outlet for your set of beliefs . . . and one day you find a piece of media with some folks who are articulating what you always believed: You're not crazy, you're right, this is exactly how the world works, and you're getting screwed."[22] (Texas left Chapo Trap House in 2021 to start his own podcast, which he cohosts with Briahna Joy Gray, a former Sanders campaign aide.)

Biased News and Commentary on Social Media

Biased news and commentary can also be found on social media platforms such as Facebook and Twitter. Most of these platforms started as online portals for friends to connect and share their life experiences, but over the years they have evolved into hotbeds of political commentary. Some of this occurs as people share stories that appear in their news feeds. In other instances, groups that represent themselves as being part of the news media post biased stories on their platforms.

For example, a popular Facebook group that goes by the name Right Wing describes itself as a media/news company. It maintains a blog and reports that some seventeen hundred Facebook members follow its posts. According to the blog, its main commentator is Don Purdum, whose background includes em-

ployment as a political campaign consultant. The profile that appears on the blog does not mention any experience or training in the techniques of objective news gathering. However, someone trawling casually through Facebook who comes across the page for Right Wing might accept the group's assertion that it is a legitimate and professional provider of objective news. A recent post on the group's Facebook page suggests otherwise. The site reported that Democratic Party leaders support granting the right to vote to unauthorized immigrants. In fact, legislators in some states as well as leaders of some city governments have backed proposals to permit *legal* immigrants who are residents of those communities the right to vote. None of those proposals would extend the right to vote to people who have entered the country illegally.

Regardless of the potential for seeing biased news on social media— whether these are stories funneled through news feeds, shared by friends, or obtained directly from a group's platform—social media as a source of news remains immensely popular. According to a 2021 study by the Pew Research Center, 53 percent of Americans rely to some degree on social media platforms for their news. Moreover, even though more than half of Americans regularly look to social media for updates on the news, the Pew study found that 59 percent of those readers doubt the accuracy of what they are reading. Concluded the Pew study, "Most Americans do not say news on social media has helped them better understand current events."[23] And yet social media is as popular as ever as a source of news— biased or not.

CHAPTER FOUR

Changing People's Perceptions About the Media

Biases are a fact of life. All people have them. Biases, the ones we know about and the ones we do not, influence how we look at and interact with people and the world around us. This is as true for journalists as it is for anyone else. But there are times when the perception of bias is even greater than the reality. Comments from politicians who are unhappy with coverage of their actions and policies are largely to blame for these perceptions. This is not a new phenomenon. In the late 1960s and early 1970s, President Richard Nixon often railed against media coverage of his management of the war in Vietnam—although he frequently dispatched his vice president, Spiro Agnew, to carry the fight. In a speech given in Des Moines, Iowa, on November 13, 1969, Agnew targeted the press, declaring that a tiny faction of American news executives decides on its own how to portray important events, including the prosecution of a war. "The purpose of my remarks tonight is to focus your attention on this little group of men who not only enjoy a right of instant rebuttal to every Presidential address, but, more importantly, wield a free hand in selecting, presenting, and interpreting the great issues in our nation,"[24] Agnew told his audience that night.

Later, Nixon is said to have told Henry Kissinger, who served as his secretary of state, "Never forget, the press is the enemy, the press is the enemy. Write that on the blackboard 100 times."[25]

The Birth of Fake News

Politicians in more recent times have carried on the tradition of berating the news media for coverage they do not like, often citing bias as a centerpiece of their complaints. Sarah Palin is among the politicians who have accused the media of bias. In 2008 Palin—then the governor of Alaska—was tapped by Republican presidential candidate John McCain to be his running mate. The McCain-Palin ticket was ultimately unsuccessful. The 2008 election was won by Democratic presidential candidate Barack Obama and his running mate, Joe Biden—at the time a US senator from Delaware.

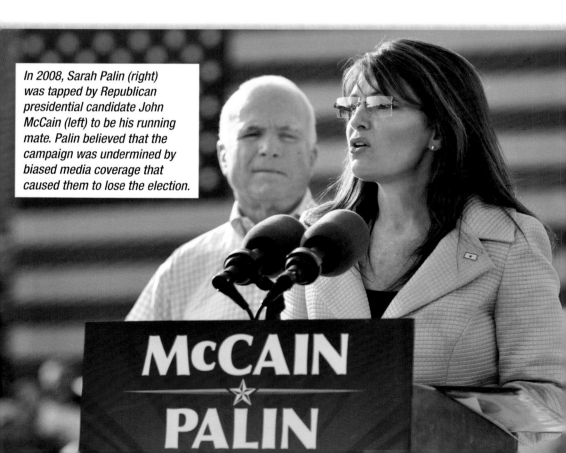

In 2008, Sarah Palin (right) was tapped by Republican presidential candidate John McCain (left) to be his running mate. Palin believed that the campaign was undermined by biased media coverage that caused them to lose the election.

Palin bristled at the loss, believing her quest for national office was undermined by the news reporters who covered her as she campaigned across the country. In 2009 she referred to journalists as the "lamestream media."[26] It was a pun she concocted, based on the phrase "mainstream media" that is often used to describe the major newspapers, magazines, and radio and TV networks that cover national stories. Palin said in 2009:

> We must always remember the big picture. The media has always been biased. Conservatives—and especially conservative women—have always been held to a different standard and attacked. Let's just acknowledge that commonsense conservatives must be stronger and work that much harder because of the obvious bias. And let's be encouraged with a sense of poetic justice by knowing that the "mainstream" media isn't mainstream anymore. That's why I call it "lamestream."[27]

Palin's anger against the media was likely prompted by press reports of dysfunction within her campaign for vice president. Following the 2008 election, Palin hoped to make a bid for the party's presidential nomination in 2012. But her presidential ambitions soon stumbled—due largely to the same type of ills that plagued her run for vice president. Reported the website Politico, which focuses on coverage of national political news:

> According to multiple Republican campaign sources, the former Alaska governor wreaks havoc on campaign logistics and planning. She offers little notice about her availability, refuses to do certain events, is obsessive about press

45

coverage, and sometimes backs out with as little lead time as she gave in the first place. In short, her seat-of-the-pants operation can be a nightmare to deal with, which, in part, explains why Palin often does not do GOP events.[28]

Palin reacted harshly to the Politico story. She appeared as a guest on a national radio show hosted by Glenn Beck—long regarded as among the most biased of right-wing broadcast commentators—to slam Jonathan Martin, the Politico reporter who wrote the story. Said Palin, "Hey, you can lie about me Politico, Jonathan Martin, ya punk. You guys can lie about me, but you're takin' on the big guns, you're takin' on Beck. You know, you're an idiot if you take 'em on!"[29]

Discrediting the Press

In the years since Palin declared war on the press, complaints of biased news coverage have escalated. Many politicians, chief among them former president Donald Trump, have branded the news media as purveyors of "fake news." While in office, Trump used the term often to accuse journalists of presenting biased news accounts of his decisions and administration's policies. "The media is really, the word, one of the greatest of all terms I've come up with, is 'fake,'" Trump said in 2017. "And it's a shame. And they really hurt the country. Because they take away the spirit of the country."[30]

Throughout his presidency, Trump never let up in his attacks on the press. In 2019 he posted this message on his Twitter account: "The press is doing everything within their power to fight the magnificence of the phrase, Make America Great Again! They can't stand the fact that this Administration has done more than virtually any other Administration in its first two years. They are truly the enemy of the people!" He would go on to slam the *New York Times*, calling the newspaper "fake and dishonest," as well as the *Washington Post*, which he referred to as "crazed and dis-

The Value of Journalism School

Bloggers, podcasters, and social media stars do not need a college degree in journalism to offer news to their readers, but if a young person aspires to a job at a newspaper, broadcast news outlet, or legitimate internet news site, a degree in journalism is regarded as a requirement. According to the website *U.S. News & World Report*, which ranks the quality of college degree programs, 356 universities in America offer degrees in journalism. Typically, journalism students take classes in newswriting, which provides guidance in not only how to write stories but also where to find the reliable information that is used to build the stories. Classes may also include courses in ethics—guidance for students in how to avoid bias in reporting their stories. Says Melissa DiPento, a journalism instructor at Brooklyn College in New York City:

> Students in journalism classes must constantly process information, form opinions on what they've heard, ask questions and share reflections. . . . They also pitch ideas and present them—often in front of their peers—which acclimates them to speaking in groups, asking questions, solving problems and much more. Feedback can be critical at times, and students find ways to accept it and adjust. Students who do well in journalism school, I believe, are truly ready to take on whatever life throws at them.

Quoted in Jessica Lawlor, "Is Journalism School Worth It? Three Journalists Weigh In," Muck Rack, December 12, 2018. https://muckrack.com.

honest."[31] This despite the fact that both newspapers have won dozens of awards for exceptional reporting, including (numerous times) journalism's highest honor: the Pulitzer Prize.

Trump's anger toward the press fired up after the US Department of Justice initiated an investigation into interference in the 2016 presidential election. The investigation found that Russian agents had planted false stories about Trump's opponent, Democrat Hillary Clinton, in social media posts. Many conservative Facebook groups and other social media platforms treated the phony stories as fact. The US Department of Justice investigation looked into whether Trump's campaign team assisted the Russian agents, ultimately determining there was no clear evidence suggesting Trump or his campaign aides conspired with the foreign agents to plant the phony stories about Clinton.

The developments in the investigation were regularly in the news, prompting Trump to lash out at the media outlets that reported them. When asked by journalist Lesley Stahl of CBS News why he constantly waged war on the press, Trump replied, "I do it to discredit you all and demean you all so when you write negative stories about me, no one will believe you."[32] That strategy seems to have worked. In a 2017 Politico/Morning Consult poll, 46 percent of voters said they believe that major news organizations fabricate stories about Trump. This view of the media has grown over time—and it has not been limited to stories about the former president. According to a 2020 Pew Research Center poll, 69 percent of respondents believed the media was exaggerating the risks of the COVID-19 pandemic. This echoed a frequent criticism leveled by Trump, who feared a public backlash caused by the pandemic could hurt his chances for reelection in 2020. "We now have some of the best news organizations that the world has known," said Paul Steiger, former editor of the *Wall Street Journal*. "But Trump has created a climate in which the best news, most fact-checked news is not being believed by many people."[33]

Dismissing Baseless Allegations

Politicians who seek to undermine the credibility of the press may have an ally in the press itself. Lester Holt, the longtime anchor of *NBC Nightly News*, suggests that when the media report outlandish claims made by politicians and other influential people, those ideas spread and take root. This, he says, does not have to happen. Providing all sides to the story does not necessarily mean giving opportunities to political leaders and others to spew outlandish and clearly false versions of events.

Holt points to the January 6, 2021, riot at the US Capitol, which was sparked by the claims of Trump and his allies that the 2020 election had been stolen from the Republican president. Numerous investigations conducted in several states by elections officials found no evidence of this. Still, when legitimate media outlets reported accusations of a stolen election, many news consumers were likely led to believe they were true.

If, on the other hand, journalists had quickly dismissed those baseless allegations and not included them in their reports, Holt argues, the story of the allegedly stolen election would have lost traction very quickly. "Providing an open platform for misinformation for anyone to come and say whatever they want, especially when issues of public health and safety are at stake can be quite dangerous," he says. "Our duty is to be fair to the truth . . . we

Throughout his presidency, Donald Trump never let up in his attacks on the press. He regularly claimed that the highly regarded New York Times was dishonest.

Uncovering the Watergate Scandal

When the *Washington Post* began publishing articles about the scandal known as Watergate, President Richard Nixon immediately accused the newspaper of biased reporting. Despite those accusations, the newspaper stood by the reporting done by Bob Woodward and Carl Bernstein. Their investigation is regarded by media experts as one of American journalism's finest moments. The scandal first came to light in June 1972 when burglars were caught by police inside the offices of the Democratic National Committee (DNC) in the Watergate, a complex of hotel rooms and offices in downtown Washington, DC. Woodward and Bernstein soon revealed that the burglars had not broken into the DNC headquarters to steal money or office equipment. Their objective was to plant electronic listening devices to gather intelligence on the Democratic candidates who planned to oppose Nixon's reelection. Moreover, the reporting by the *Washington Post* revealed that the Watergate burglars were acting under the direction of Nixon's campaign committee and aides on the president's White House staff.

The revelations reported in the newspaper led to congressional investigations. Those investigations eventually led to Nixon's decision to resign the presidency in 1974. The *Washington Post* was awarded the 1973 Pulitzer Prize—the highest honor conferred on American journalism—for the work done by Woodward and Bernstein.

need to hear our leaders' views, their policies and reasoning. It's really important. But we have to stand ready to push back and call out falsehoods."[34]

Ethics Guidelines

Actual bias and perceived bias can both damage the credibility of the news media. For this reason, many news organizations have developed standards of ethical behavior. These standards seek to minimize bias, ensure fairness, and eliminate conflicts of interest among journalists at all levels. The ethics policy of the *Washington Post*, for instance, covers the importance of reporters remaining objective in how they craft their stories, including the requirement to interview participants with differing viewpoints. It also includes a lengthy section on fairness, which reads:

Reporters and editors of the *Post* are committed to fairness. While arguments about objectivity are endless, the concept of fairness is something that editors and reporters can easily understand and pursue. Fairness results from a few simple practices: No story is fair if it omits facts of major importance or significance. Fairness includes completeness.

No story is fair if it includes essentially irrelevant information at the expense of significant facts. Fairness includes relevance.

No story is fair if it consciously or unconsciously misleads or even deceives the reader. Fairness includes honesty— leveling with the reader.

No story is fair if it covers individuals or organizations that have not been given the opportunity to address assertions or claims about them made by others. Fairness includes diligently seeking comment and taking that comment genuinely into account.[35]

Other media organizations have instituted similar standards, often providing direct instructions to reporters on how to handle certain situations. For example, the ethics guidelines established by the *Los Angeles Times* require reporters to make every effort possible to contact people who are portrayed in an adverse light in the paper's stories so that they have the opportunity to explain or defend their actions or views. Specifically, the *Times*'s ethics guidelines require reporters to seek face-to-face meetings to obtain these comments rather than calling or emailing. This is not just a random request. In-person conversations can enhance the reporter's understanding of that person's background, intentions, and motivations—all of which result in a more balanced account. "Reporting requires special diligence with respect to fairness," state the ethics standards published by the *Los Angeles Times*. "Those involved in such work should bear in mind that they are more credible when they provide a rich, nuanced account of the topic. Our coverage should avoid simplistic portrayals."[36]

CBS News has set standards for its journalists that go beyond how they craft their stories for the networks' newscasts. For example, the network has prohibited its news staff members from making financial donations to political campaigns. Across America, many voters send money to campaign committees established to finance the campaigns of individual candidates. And it is not unusual for campaign committees supporting candidates for statewide or national offices to rake in millions of dollars to buy advertising, hire campaign aides, conduct polling, and provide all the other services required to launch campaigns for public office. However, employees of CBS News are prohibited from providing financial support for candidates. "We want our reporters to be absolutely pure when they interview candidates of either side or issues that relate to either side," says Linda Mason, vice president of CBS News. "Today, with the instant reporting of political contributions, it has become obvious who gives and to whom, and this we felt would compromise the people who were doing reporting involved with political issues."[37]

Los Angeles Times *ethics guidelines require reporters to make every effort possible to contact people who are portrayed in an adverse light in the publisher's stories so that they have the opportunity to defend themselves.*

Moreover, when CBS News journalists perform work away from their duties at the network—perhaps by giving speeches, publishing books, or writing op-ed columns for newspapers—that work must receive approval from senior management at the network before it can be made public. And, Mason makes it clear, if that outside work dives into the political sphere, the senior management at CBS News is not likely to approve it. "That's so that, again, your opinions don't reflect badly on CBS, or in any way show bias towards one side or the other,"[38] Mason says.

> "We want our reporters to be absolutely pure when they interview candidates of either side or issues that relate to either side."[37]
>
> —Linda Mason, vice president of CBS News

Ongoing Challenges

The job of reporting the news is an essential aspect of American democracy. The challenge for the media is, as ever, to strive for fair, accurate, timely, and unbiased reporting. Nearly twenty-one thousand Americans were engaged in this endeavor in 2020, according to the US Department of Labor. This number includes reporters, editors, photographers, camera operators, producers, sound engineers, data analysts, and others who individually and collectively bring news and information to millions of readers, listeners, and viewers.

These professionals face many challenges. Constantly being aware of their own biases is one of these challenges. Respected news organizations work hard to make sure they recognize bias within their own ranks. This is a worthy goal. Says William David Sloan, a professor of journalism history at the University of Alabama, "Why is it important that the news media be fair, balanced, and unbiased? If we believe that the media are important to American democracy, then the answer is obvious. For the system to work, we must have a well-informed citizenry."[39]

SOURCE NOTES

Introduction: Media Bias and the Trial of Kyle Rittenhouse

1. Quoted in Ken Meyer, "Ingraham Defends Alleged Murderer Kyle Rittenhouse, Asks Why Someone Who 'Actually Defends Himself' Is Now 'the Enemy,'" Mediaite, September 1, 2020. www.mediaite.com.

2. David A. Love, "White Domestic Terrorists like Kyle Rittenhouse Are Held to a Different Standard," Yahoo!, November 20, 2020. www.yahoo.com.

3. Henry A. Brechter, "Media Bias Alert: How Left and Right Media Are Covering the Rittenhouse Trial," AllSides, November 11, 2021. www.allsides.com.

Chapter One: News, Opinion, and Bias, How Do They Differ?

4. Carrie Seidman, "Understanding the Difference Between Commentary and News," *Daytona Beach (FL) News-Journal*, June 23, 2019. www.news-journalonline.com.

5. Quoted in Dylan Byers, "Rep. Ellison Explodes on Fox News, Calls Sean Hannity 'Worst Excuse for a Journalist,'" Politico, February 26, 2013. www.politico.com.

6. Quoted in UT Life, "The Root of Media Bias," January 4, 2016. www.ut.edu.

7. Quoted in Media Matters for America, *Tucker Carlson's Descent into White Supremacy: A Timeline*, 2021. https://cloudfront.mediamatters.org.

8. Marshall Cohen, "Fact-Check: Fox News and Republican Lawmakers Push New False Flag Conspiracy That FBI Orchestrated US Capitol Attack," CNN, June 17, 2021. www.cnn.com.

9. Quoted in Willa Paskin, "Rachel Maddow Turned a Scoop on Donald Trump's Taxes into a Cynical, Self-Defeating Spectacle," Slate, March 15, 2017. https://slate.com.

10. Paskin, "Rachel Maddow Turned a Scoop on Donald Trump's Taxes into a Cynical, Self-Defeating Spectacle."

Chapter Two: How Does Bias Affect News Consumers?

11. Quoted in Ryan Bort, "Fox News' Anti-vaccination Hysteria Has Reached a Disturbing New Level," *Rolling Stone*, July 9, 2021. www.rollingstone.com.

12. Quoted in Denise Robbins, "Analysis: How Michigan and National Reporters Covered the Flint Water Crisis," Media Matters for America, February 1, 2016. www.mediamatters.org.

13. Quoted in Yessenia Funes, "New Harvard Analysis Highlights How Media Failed the People of Flint," Colorlines, July 11, 2017. www.colorlines.com.

14. Anti-Defamation League, "Alex Jones: Five Things to Know," 2021. www.adl.org.

15. Quoted in Gerrard Kaonga, "Tucker Carlson Defends Alex Jones, Says He Is Better than Other Journalists," *Newsweek*, December 2, 2021. www.newsweek.com.

16. Quoted in Michael E. Miller, "The Pizzagate Gunman Is Out of Prison. Conspiracy Theories Are Out of Control," *Seattle Times*, February 16, 2021. www.seattletimes.com.

Chapter Three: Bias in the New Media

17. Quoted in Tyler O'Neil, "President Biden Refers to VP Kamala Harris as 'First Lady,'" Fox News, March 15, 2022. www.foxnews.com.

18. Sophie O'Hara, "Jill Biden to the Rescue Again . . . She Has to Jump in and Save Joe," Wayne Dupree, March 16, 2022. https://waynedupree.com.

19. Glen Reaux, "Republican Party Suicidal, Stupid, Insane or Something Else?," Xplicit News, May 25, 2021. www.xplicitnews.org.

20. Paul Thornton, "Opinion Newsletter: On Comparing Trump to Hitler and Mussolini," *Los Angeles Times*, July 25, 2020. www.latimes.com.

21. Aaron Wall, "Is Your Blog Biased?," *ProBlogger*, April 9, 2007. https://problogger.com.

22. Quoted in Nellie Bowles, "The Pied Pipers of the Dirtbag Left Want to Lead Everyone to Bernie Sanders," *New York Times*, March 1, 2020, p. A-1.

23. Elisa Shearer and Amy Mitchell, "News Use Across Social Media Platforms in 2020," Pew Research Center, January 12, 2021. www.pewresearch.org.

24. Quoted in Otterbein University, "Vice President Spiro Agnew Speech at Des Moines, Iowa: November 13, 1969," April 4, 2021. www.otterbein.edu.

25. Quoted in Matt Giles, "When Richard Nixon Declared War on the Media," Longreads, November 8, 2018. https://longreads.com.

26. Quoted in Nick Wing, "Sarah Palin Goes on Offense Against Lamestream Media: 'Reload or White Flag?,'" HuffPost, March 25, 2011. www.huffpost.com.

27. Quoted in Wing, "Sarah Palin Goes on Offense Against Lamestream Media."

28. Quoted in Geoffrey Dunn, *The Lies of Sarah Palin: The Untold Story Behind Her Relentless Quest for Power*. New York: St. Martin's, 2011, p. 407.

29. Quoted in Dunn, *The Lies of Sarah Palin*, p. 407.

30. Quoted in Chris Cillizza, "Donald Trump Just Claimed He Invented 'Fake News,'" CNN, October 26, 2017. www.cnn.com.

31. Quoted in Brett Samuels, "Trump Ramps Up Rhetoric on Media, Calls Press 'the Enemy of the People,'" *The Hill* (Washington, DC), April 5, 2019. https://thehill.com.

32. Quoted in Dean Obeidallah, "Media Isn't Partisan. Democrats Need to Stop Claiming It Is," MSNBC, December 6, 2021. www.msnbc.com.

33. Quoted in Committee to Protect Journalists, "The Trump Administration and the Media," April 16, 2020. https://cpj.org.

34. Quoted in Dominick Mastrangelo, "NBC's Lester Holt Warns Media Against Giving 'Platform for Misinformation,'" *The Hill* (Washington, DC), March 32, 2021. https://thehill.com.

35. *Washington Post*, "Policies and Standards," 2021. www.washingtonpost.com.

36. *Los Angeles Times*, "*Los Angeles Times* Ethics Guidelines," June 16, 2014. www.latimes.com.

37. Quoted in Brian Montopoli, "New Standards for CBS News," CBS News, October 9, 2006. www.cbsnews.com.

38. Quoted in Montopoli, "New Standards for CBS News."

39. William David Sloan and Jenn Burleson Mackay, eds., *Media Bias: Finding It, Fixing It*. Jefferson, NC: McFarland, 2007, p. 8.

FOR FURTHER RESEARCH

Books

Jerry Ceppos, ed., *Covering Politics in the Age of Trump*. Baton Rouge: Louisiana State University Press, 2021.

Sue Ellen Christian, *Overcoming Bias: A Journalist's Guide to Culture & Context*. New York: Routledge, 2021.

Stephanie Craft and Charles Davis, *Principles of American Journalism*. New York: Routledge, 2021.

Brian Stelter, *Hoax: Donald Trump, Fox News, and the Dangerous Distortion of Truth*. New York: One Signal, 2020.

Matt Taibbi, *Hate, Inc.: Why Today's Media Makes Us Despise One Another*. New York: OR Books, 2021.

Internet Sources

Ryan Bort, "Fox News' Anti-vaccination Hysteria Has Reached a Disturbing New Level," *Rolling Stone*, July 9, 2021. www.rollingstone.com.

Committee to Protect Journalists, "The Trump Administration and the Media," April 16, 2020. https://cpj.org.

Dominick Mastrangelo, "NBC's Lester Holt Warns Media Against Giving 'Platform for Misinformation,'" *The Hill* (Washington, DC), March 32, 2021. https://thehill.com.

Brett Samuels, "Trump Ramps Up Rhetoric on Media, Calls Press 'The Enemy of the People,'" *The Hill* (Washington, DC), April 5, 2019. https://thehill.com.

Carrie Seidman, "Understanding the Difference Between Commentary and News," *Daytona Beach (FL) News-Journal*, June 23, 2019. www.news-journalonline.com.

Marc Tracy, "Top Editor of *Philadelphia Inquirer* Resigns After 'Buildings Matter' Headline," *New York Times*, June 6, 2020. www.nytimes.com.

Websites

Allsides

www.allsides.com

This website was established in 2012 with the goal of identifying bias. It posts news stories, providing examples created by right-leaning news platforms, left-leaning news platforms, and news platforms that provide objective versions of the stories. By reading all three versions, readers can detect the degree of bias in each story.

Fairness & Accuracy in Reporting

https://fair.org

This New York City–based group serves as a watchdog, flagging news organizations it finds to be biased. By accessing the tab for CounterSpin Radio, visitors to the organization's website can listen to recordings of a weekly radio show, hosted by journalist Janine Jackson, in which she discusses examples of bias she finds in current news reporting.

Politifact

www.politifact.com

Politifact assesses whether comments made by political leaders that have been reported in the news media contain factual information. The comments and the news organizations that publish them are given grades by Politifact. A review of Politifact assessments finds that most blogs are given grades of "fail" when it comes to providing fact-based comments for readers.

Poynter Institute

www.poynter.org

Located in St. Petersburg, Florida, the Poynter Institute supports efforts to maintain objective journalism. By accessing the MediaWise tab on the Poynter Institute website, visitors can find the Teen Fact-Checking Network, which selects top stories in the news and assesses their factual content for young readers.

Pulitzer Prize

www.pulitzer.org

The Pulitzer Prize is the top award conferred each year on journalism produced by American print and internet platforms. By accessing the Pulitzer website, visitors can find the news stories and columns judged to be the best, and most objective, examples of journalism in America.

RECOGNIZING BIAS

The news media has a responsibility to be fair, accurate, and balanced in its reporting on topics large and small. Many members of the media strive to do just that. Others do not. For this reason, news consumers also need to be vigilant when reading, viewing, or listening to news reports. Here are some ways to determine whether news content is biased.

Does the story have a spin?

Spin is a term applied to news stories that are slanted to favor one side. (Public relations professionals employed by celebrities, corporations, and politicians are known as "spin doctors"—it is their job to get journalists to do stories that are favorable to their clients.) Watch for stories that contain language or draw conclusions that favor one side over another.

Who is quoted in the story?

Whether news or commentary, spokespersons for both sides of an issue should be quoted. Or an attempt to reach both sides should at least be noted. Stories based on a single source, without any attempt to seek out the other side, are likely to be biased.

How are adjectives and nouns used in the story?

News reports can leave different impressions simply by the choice of nouns and adjectives. A news report that describes participants in a protest as "lawless hooligans" will leave a different impression than one that describes the participants as "fervent protesters."

Is the reporter qualified to report the news?

Check the credentials of the person reporting the news. Does the reporter have a journalism degree or any background in the techniques of objective news gathering? Does the reporter have any expertise in the subject area on which he or she is reporting? This is not always the case, but it can be another way to determine credibility.

What is the angle of the story?

Angle refers to the main thrust of a news story. In reporting on a hurricane, the storm's destruction would normally be the focus, or angle. In political coverage, there could be various angles—some of which indicate bias. A story that focuses exclusively on damage resulting from a public protest would suggest bias against the protesters. A story that focuses on the reasons for the protest, as well as the aftermath, presents a more balanced view of the event.

Who are the sources cited in the story?

People who work for the government or large corporations often serve as authorities for topics reporters may be writing about. Other sources often hold different views. A balanced story will feature interviews with authorities as well as others who have different perspectives.

Is the story supported by the facts?

Fair and unbiased news reporting depends on accurate facts and documentation. If a reporter or commentator makes assertions or draws conclusions but provides no facts or documentation to support those statements, it is a sign of bias.

Are opinions presented as facts?

Opinion is a legitimate part of news as long as it is clearly labeled as such. Not all news organizations make that distinction. Facts can be verified as either true or false. Opinions express beliefs, attitudes, and judgments; they are not true or false. To spot opinion masquerading as fact, look for words that cannot be verified or measured such as best, worst, wonderful, and disgusting.

INDEX

PICTURE CREDITS